Stormwatcher
A view from the inside
by
David G Kelly

Dedication

This book is dedicated to those that have walked the road of mental health either as a supporter or sufferer, to those still marching onward, to those that have found victory and to those that left the fight to early.
It is also dedicated to those of my family and friends that did not desert me even in my most irrational and darkest of days. I can never thank you enough for your understanding, [even when you didn't understand], your love and your giving of time to what often felt at least in my head as a lost cause. To my Saviour whose words I held on to.

Foreword

Having travelled the road of mental health as a psychiatric assistant and therapist, a supporter and ongoing combatant, it is a path fraught with ups and downs, victories and losses. At certain moments there are tinges of humour and light that lead us to realise that we can go on at least for the moment.

CONTENTS

Tunnel

Standing here, if you were me,
Would you know where the light for this tunnel
would be?
Could you just open a door in the wall,
Step free from these feelings, once and for all?
Don't think that I've chosen to walk in the dark,
I assure you I'd rather take a walk in the park!
I know you just think that your trying to do right,
But my actions are not 'boredom',
I do want to fight!
But sometimes the only release I can find,
To escape from the darkness that's filling my mind
Is cleansing, releasing a small part of me,
It's something that's real and something to see
So think before speaking, consider the mark
See if it's so easy to escape from the dark.

The Host

'LISTEN' can't you hear them?
Sitting on my bed,
A host of 'living' dead men are talking in my head
What is it that they want of me?
Did I 'invite' them in?
Of course I didn't stupid,
please get them off my skin!
They try to take my voice away,
They hold it like a vice,
I'll get you BASTARDS off of me,
No matter what the price!
They don't want the medication,
Cos' they don't want to leave,
But I'm not a 'living' dead man,
NO! my name is Steve
So bring in the drugs and the Psych,
Lets see what they can do,
Cos now the battles starting,
I want my life anew.

Hands

Looking at this pair of hands,
Tell me what you see,
They have so many uses,
Oh what could that be?
They could choose to be destructive,
Guided from within,
A piece of glass, a coke can ring,
To cut away my skin
They could wash and wash and wash and wash
And wash again once more,
Washing, washing, washing,
Till my skins it glows red raw
And then I hear 'do it again'
'You know you need to clean',
'FUCK OFF!' I shout 'YOU BASTARD'
To this hidden voice unseen
For somewhere deep inside my head,
There's a 'voice' a 'tick'
That really just won't stop,
Sometimes my will seems futile,
Give up, go on, just drop!'
NO! I WON'T, I WILL GO ON,
That's the story my life must tell
For I have decided its time to ride and head
For the land called 'WELL'
So bear with me please and now and then
Allow for me to fall,
And then one day I'll walk with you,
HEALED, PROUD and TALL.

The Man in the Moon

Today I saw the man in the moon
But guess what, that man, he was asleep
Quiet, peaceful, serenity's womb,
In a field of black velvet deep
I thought I'd like to wake him
And ask him how it's done?
To live within his darkness,
And yet still see the sun
Cos' sometimes I can't do it,
All I see is the black,
I try and try to reach the sun
But something holds me back
It's like a force, unseen, untouched
That dictates life, its rules,
And yet allows me brief moments
Building my hopes 'you fool'
Call it depression or what you will
A name won't ease the pain,
Just let me, like him, know that word
That you, and the world, call 'SANE!'

A Companion for Life?

To feel the world is oh so close
It breathing down your neck,
To be aware of every breath
And you can't say 'what the heck!'
To no longer be aware of space
Perspective lost or a fading trace?
To walk and know sensations face
When he's not really at my door
So, is that really touching me?
Did it just touch my hem?
Do I need to wash again to be free of 'them'
But if I do it, if I give in
Just who is it that can say 'I WIN'
Will it be all of the thoughts,
That will forever rule my life?
Or will they finally walk with me
Like a loving wife
Oh God I hope it's the latter, a companion for life

Stainless Steel

There I see you shiny, There I see you clean
You have so many uses, You know what I mean
But when you came into this world,
Your purpose pre-ordained
Did you think that 'one fine day',
You'd lie all bloodied and stained?
But then you see your not like me,
For my scars still remain
They speak each day of anguish felt,
And how I 'deal' with pain
One scar for hurt and one for spite,
And two for angers voice
You've helped me to do this to myself,
And yet you had no choice
But rest in the thought that one day,
I may not need you to help me feel
Then in memories locked and shiny state,
Once more you will be....
Stainless steel.

Let me out, Help me out

Let me out, let me out!
Why can't you bastards see?
This great big wall that's standing here,
Between both you and me
Can't you see me pushing?
My face hard against the stone
I claw so hard to get through,
My fingers are torn to the bone
That sometimes seems at least to me,
Not good enough for you!
You pull and pull and pull again
To try and drag me through
And yes within this world it seems
That all revolves round me,
And if I admit it, its sometimes true,
It's so much 'easier' you see
Oh what am I saying!
To be like this makes my issues a tomb,
Just help me break the wall down
Escape from this unwanted womb
I don't just want glimpses of life, no future,
Then a quick glimpse of sun!
You can see when I'm trying,
I hate being comfortably numb
So don't give up on me, all of you please!
As a PD I know I'm hard work!
Keep checking the brickwork
Find the issues that bind
Help me see the wood for the trees!

Mother?

Have you ever stopped to consider?
What you do to me
By bringing with you those foul men,
Who I would rather never see!
After all your not innocent,
You know and know what they did
Where was the wing of a Mothers love
When I run and hid?
Although they say that time it heals
Well with my scars its true
But here within my aching head
I can't stop it coming through
Those great big hands, that heavy breath,
A fate I now consider worse
Than my impending death
It seems to me a small price to pay,
A Zebra skin all torn,
For what use am I to anyone,
Battered, bruised and worn
But even this is harder now,
As restraint is part of my life,
And will I ever recover enough?
To be a mother, a lover, a wife?
Its not an impossibility
I will once more control my life,
But please think of me next time I see you!
My fathers 'trouble and strife'

Consider This

Have you ever considered what it is like
To look back on life at your deeds,
Consider where your standing now
And the terror just standing now feeds.
Have you ever considered a walk in the park
A thing of joy and delight
And how you'd feel if you were me
It's like the emptiness of night,
To always and constantly be so well aware
Of each tiny movement, a leaf in the air
To have your head pounding
With thoughts you don't need
Growing and growing like an invading weed
Relieved at the thought of one step without pain,
But now, I must step, again and again
And I know it goes on
like this till I'm home,
Safe and entombed like a pharaoh in stone!

Wave upon Wave

Wave upon wave it takes over me,
I'm like King Canute and his conquering sea
Demanding, Commanding, retreat and take heed,
Can't you just for once listen
And let me have what I need
I need to take my mind back
Like Canute demanded his land,
But it was God who commanded the sea
So why wont he give 'ME' a hand?
I know sometimes its subtle ways
In which the hand of God it moves,
But now and then in my relentless state,
in the more obvious I'd like him to prove
I'm not saying that I don't believe
And yes it was choice that led me this far,
But a miracle is sorely needed Lord,
Not just a guiding 'star'

So Much More

An open hand,
A hard clenched fist
Time to myself,
Not one chance missed
The need to see a bloodied mark,
To find release from all this dark
And yet the light that my actions bring,
Still don't cause my heart to sing
I'm like an iceberg, so much hid,
A game of chess, an ignored kid.

Should Be

To dance a dance on powdered wings,
To hear a song that angels sing
To know the joy that each day brings,
Is how my life should be.
To feel the spray of an ocean blue,
To know my love for you is true
To grab life's gifts, not miss the cue,
Is how my life should be.
And as I look and wonder how,
It's then I focus here and now
It's time to put my hand to the plow,
To get to where my life should be.

Release

To want release and yet stay bound,
To ways of coping I have found
Like a rock face scarred and worn,
From this world you'd have me torn
There's so much energy put into this,
And yet release would bring me bliss
For then I could stand and 'admire' the view,
Of all the things I've put us through
The highs, the lows, the in-between,
Of things I did and you've not seen
For, yes there's more than on this wall,
A life long tale of my rise and fall
Miracles are instant, life takes more time,
Don't offer a penny for them,
They're surely worth a dime.

Last Night

Last night a star was in the sky,
Just like a twinkle in Gods eye
He looked at me and wondered why?
I seemed so all alone.
He had to agree that my life was rough,
And what I'd been through did seem tough
But said "don't you think you've put yourself through
enough"?
It's time to make a change.
Yes you feel anger, and certainly pain,
But don't keep disfiguring again and again
You're a child in a big world with so much to gain,
Grab life and live it anew.
He then bid goodnight, and left with my thoughts,
I considered his words the lessons it taught
But the choice is mine; will it result in naught?
I don't know but it's time to decide!

Storm Watcher

Today I felt the storm rise,
I felt it in my bones
The gentle thunder rising,
In soft deep throated groans
It's coming, I can't stop it,
Foundations feel the change,
1, 2, 3, 4 its coming into range
I can feel it rising, winds surround my knees,
Thoughts of changing weathers is all that my eye sees
Waters start a rushing flowing in swirling mood,
The storm now even closer,
Unleashing thoughts accrued
I feel it now much deeper,
The swirling pools made known,
Engulfing me within its grip!
But through these storms I've grown
The storms now moving higher,
High winds they take my breath
It's a force I feel within my chest
Like all impending death!
My voice is lost upon the back of this primeval force,
Wave upon wave of natures grip,
Has almost run its course
And soon the storm is waning,
Yet goose leather and hairs still stand
As the finally visible reminders,
Of the storms that have ravaged this land.

Walk the Walk

I tried to walk the walk today,
Instead I talked the walk
Though a simple journey, merely A to B,
I tread a narrow pathway and still it makes me balk
The walls of stone though 6ft gone,
Appear no further than an inch
The cactus that I walk past,
Though silent and still makes me flinch
To move between these places,
My hands are drawn right up
I grasp my mouth with fingers,
Like a man without a cup
These motions that I go through,
Exaggerate at different times of life
Why can't I just have a life of constant,
Instead of calm, to anxious, to strife.

Therapy

Today we offered therapy,
In return they offered apathy
What is it with these people that I see?
They lay in bed 'til after noon,
If it were possible be fed with a spoon
It's a whole host of servants they need, 'not me'
To work with those psychotic,
In a world almost hypnotic
I accept, understand that its hard
For those just too lazy,
It's really driving me crazy
To understand why they don't play this card
Though Therapy is admittedly not all,
I believe it could lead to a curtain call
And finally end their stay.

Psychotic Episode

I'm having a psychotic episode,
Today I feel just fine
Don't need my medication now,
See, I can walk the line
Don't want to chase a singing star,
An autographs just fine
But thoughts they come and vaguely go,
They all don't seem to be mine
Cos yesterday I walked the hall,
To pick up paying fares
With so many paying customers,
I try to make my share
From this extreme to I'm scared of snakes,
Are there any nearby I ask
Not for miles around I'm told,
That's good, my fear has passed
I know this seems so jumbled,
It's like my head you see
Flying here and jumping there,
But folks it's only 'me'

Its Time

I think it's time to say this
YES it really is the time!
I've tried so hard to forgive
But I'm sorry, the following time is mine!
I know your gone, your stone cold dead
But in just a few hours YOU 'fucked up my head!'
I should have followed my instinct
Not tripped with you around!
I should have known you weren't a friend
For your gain you'd run me into the ground
You purposely chose to confuse me
To freak me out for fun
You lousy shit, you bastard, you toe rag
Less than scum!
I accept my side of the moment
But till you, all had been safe
Then for a moment of pleasure you destroyed my life
It started so insidious, it crept up unawares
Building my insanity slowly
Like a thief that climbs the stairs
He worked his way into my head till he dogged my
every breath
Taking me close to distraction,
would I at points welcomed death?
And you see that thief is still with me
20 years come and gone
20 years of shadows, I slowly lost the sun
I'm not sure if I'll ever see it shining full
Walk in its light without fear
I know you've been dead as long now
But your legacy still walks near!

Could your drug-induced death have been so
eventful?
As my daily walk in life,
and my companion named 'fear!'

The Ward

Have you ever wondered what it must be like
To walk through that doorway
And then to spend the night
But then to let it in your mind
Your stay is not that brief
It's not a thought I think you'd cherish,
More likely give you grief
For in the minds of many, you need a ward secure
A turnkey lock, a coded pad, no leaving from the
floor
I know you think that you are well
You're held against your will
But take your time and trust me
Please, come on, just take the pill.

Around the table

We sit around the table
With many thoughts one task
Are they private? Are they free?
Should I dare to ask?
For there within this circle
I see an outward sign
Of scars that lie so deep within
Are any just like mine?
We all have carried burdens
Not always on our own
They come from life and living
And with some help we've grown
But still there's those that take more time
Hard lessons still not won
And I can see the troubled brow
The arms, the marks, fresh done
But persevere and keep on
Support it lies just here
In writing and in talking
And in those so near

One more knot

Just one more knot
It's but a turn to take my life and not return
To feel the ebb of life give way
Surrender all, let darkness stay
It's time to leave, I've done it all
Tried to face it and yet I fall
For though in walking my life is naught
Now, the solace of sleep in its web I'm caught
The thoughts pervade, invade, remind
I'm no longer able to be blind
So with no escape, what can I do?
Why not swap places let me be you
Then understand all of the things that I do
Then maybe one day when I'm all cold and blue
You'll bid me a peaceful farewell and a fond
adieu.

Don't Know

I'm just a little don't know
I'm not too sure of how to grow
I'm not too sure of how to walk
To dance or sing or even talk
How did I try to comb my hair?
Is there really any there?
Am I here or am I there?
Am I fast or am I slow?
These are just some of the questions that seem to
grow
But I can't answer them Cos I'm just a little don't know.